DON'T BE SCARED

MAGDALENA ZURAWSKI

the operating system c. 2019

the operating system digital print//document

DON'T BE SCARED

ISBN # 978-1-946031-65-5
copyright © 2019 by Magdalena Zurawski
edited and designed by ELÆ [Lynne DeSilva-Johnson] with Orchid Tierney

is released under a Creative Commons CC-BY-NC-ND (Attribution, Non Commercial, No Derivatives) License: its reproduction is encouraged for those who otherwise could not afford its purchase in the case of academic, personal, and other creative usage from which no profit will accrue.

Complete rules and restrictions are available at:
http://creativecommons.org/licenses/by-nc-nd/3.0/

For additional questions regarding reproduction, quotation, or to request a pdf for review
contact operator@theoperatingsystem.org

Print books from The Operating System are distributed to the trade by SPD/Small Press Distribution, with ePub and POD via Ingram, with production by Spencer Printing, in Honesdale, PA, in the USA. Digital books are available directly from the OS, direct from authors, via DIY pamplet printing, and/or POD.

This text was set in Steelworks Vintage, Europa-Light, Gill Sans, Minion, and OCR-A Standard.

Cover Art uses an image from "Collected Objects & the Dead Birds I Did Not Carry Home," by Heidi Reszies.

the operating system
www.theoperatingsystem.org
mailto: operator@theoperatingsystem.org

DON'T BE SCARED

for my students

On the first
day of class I told
my students not
to be scared of the
word CARTESIAN. I said it
was just a kind of
shorthand for
an idea. It was Tuesday
the second week
of August. A hot, swampy, Tuesday
in the state of Georgia, a kind of shorthand
for an idea of America. IF YOU
ONLY KNOW
ONE THING
ABOUT RENE DESCARTES, I said to them
that morning, I BET YOU KNOW
WHAT CARTESIAN MEANS.
I was
a little nervous because
I felt self-conscious. Or I felt self-conscious
because I was

a little nervous. My arms
and jokes felt heavy
and fell flat. After a little bit
of silence
someone said
with a question mark in her voice,
I THINK, THEREFORE, I AM,
and I said, YES!
On the first day of class
my sympathy
with students is abstract
because
my students are still
an abstraction. I don't know their names.
An abstracted other
makes a professor feel
heavy and flat. The class was
Twentieth-Century Poetics. I was starting
with Descartes
because the editor's introduction
used the word CARTESIAN
and I was scared
the first sentence
of the reading would make
my students think

they couldn't understand
an entire century
because they would assume
the word CARTESIAN stood for something
they didn't know,
rather than something
they did know. Abstractly speaking,
no person likes
to feel stupid. And so
I continued:
AND NOW ALL WE HAVE TO DO
IS FIGURE OUT
WHY THINKING
MIGHT PROVE TO SOMEONE
THAT SHE EXISTS.
We talked about self-consciousness,
and how we can watch ourselves think
and how when we watch ourselves think
we are both subject and object
and how the problem of modernity
in many ways is that every subject
is walking around
turning everything
into an object for himself.
HISTORY, TOO,

HAS PREFERRED PRONOUNS, I said.
(Actually, I didn't). That first day
I had consciously chosen
a linen shirt to wear
not only because it was hot, but also
to remember how I felt
somewhere else outside
of the university and outside
of the country, somewhere where
the political turmoil
wasn't mine. I wanted to know
just how foreign
home could feel. I had
bought the linen shirt
a few weeks earlier in Greece
on the island
of Hydra, where I had gone to swim
after I attended
a poetry symposium in Athens, where I had been
just a poet, not an employee
of the state of Georgia, at least not
in my mind. When I arrived
in Athens, Greece,
I said to the Greek poets, I'M FROM ATHENS,
GEORGIA. At first,

I thought this was funny
but later in a dismantled phone booth
on the sidewalk
next to the ticket booth
for the Acropolis
I saw graffiti that said,
FROM BALTIMORE TO GREECE, FUCK
THE POLICE. Gina took
a picture of this exhibit
on display in the very cradle
of democracy
because it connected
our world to the ancients. Nearby
on a large sign UNESCO
explained the Acropolis
to us in two sentences. In the first sentence
we were told that
ON THIS HILL WERE BORN
DEMOCRACY, PHILOSOPHY,
THEATER, FREEDOM OF
EXPRESSION AND SPEECH. The sentence also said
that these things were
THE INTELLECTUAL AND SPIRITUAL
FOUNDATION FOR THE CONTEMPORARY
WORLD AND ITS VALUES. The second sentence, though,

said that THE ACROPOLIS' MONUMENTS,
HAVE SURVIVED FOR ALMOST TWENTY-FIVE CENTURIES
THROUGH WARS, EXPLOSIONS, BOMBARDMENTS, FIRES, EARTHQUAKES,
SACKINGS,
INTERVENTIONS AND ALTERATIONS,
which made me think
the first sentence was
just wishful thinking,
because if democracy,
philosophy, etc. were really
the intellectual and spiritual
foundation of our
world, then there could not
have been so many EXPLOSIONS, BOMBARDMENTS, SACKINGS,
INTERVENTIONS AND ALTERATIONS trying
to destroy it. Was the copywriter
hired by UNESCO
trying to communicate
to heat-stroked tourists
that liberal democracy was an aberration,
a fragile
possibility, snuffed out
and weakened at every
possible historical turn? Was her aim
to remind us that political life

was most often
orchestrated by a will
to power backed by violence,
despite the fact that
her paid assignment
was to celebrate the Acropolis? If so, what
a genius, I thought.
And as I walked through the ruins
of democracy's spiritual and
intellectual foundation
I thought the terrain
would be an excellent example
to use with my students in explaining
Charles Olson's famous paraphrase
of Robert Creeley, FORM IS NEVER MORE
THAN AN EXTENSION OF CONTENT. Maybe twenty-five
centuries ago Robert Creeley
should have warned
the Greeks, FOR CHRIST'S SAKE,
LOOK OUT WHERE YR GOING.
When I was
a kid the classroom
was where I went
because there was
nowhere else

to go. For me, maybe
because I lack
imagination, there appeared
no other route
of escape. Sometimes now
when I'm teaching, because I am
an American, I think
about what I would
do, if someone
started shooting at my students
and me. I think
the best thing
would be for me
to walk
toward the shooter while
speaking, so that the shooter
couldn't easily abstract
me and forget I was
a real person. I always
imagine saying something
about my mother and
his mother, as if reminding him
that we each have
someone, who would weep
for us, as if remembering our

origins might help him
stop what
he's doing. The most popular semi-automatic
rifles on the market
fire 45 rounds per minute, so I probably
wouldn't get a word
out but maybe
my body could block
the shots from hitting
my students who haven't
lived as long as I have. I NEED TO GET
IN THE WAY, I tell
myself, as if it's more
necessary to preserve a natural
order than to save
my own life. I tell myself,
IT WOULD BE OK
FOR ME TO DIE. I'VE ALREADY ESCAPED.
I'M HERE. I don't know
if I would want to live after something
like that anyhow. They would have
taken my classroom away from me. When I traveled
through India with my mother,
she saw a stray dog
trying to nurse her puppies

in the gutter. My mother
got very angry when she saw
that the dog was hungry, maybe too hungry
to make milk to feed
her puppies. She demanded
the children with us
run into the kitchen and
get food
for the animal. Watching my mother
feed the dog
became one way
for me to understand her. It also
became a way for me
to think about the relationship of empathy
to action. Would my mother have demanded food
for the dog, if the dog
had had no puppies? Would she have felt
the need to feed
the dog, if my brother and I
did not exist? Would I be willing
to use my body
to block a shooter anywhere
or just in my classroom? If you go
to school long enough
you learn that modernity is just

a series of ways
the self has tried
to prove its own existence
to itself, usually in ways
that use other bodies
to do so, like if Wordsworth
sits on the grass and
looks at a tree or
a woman in a cottage
what he mostly sees is how sensitive
his own thinking about the tree
or the woman in the cottage is and
it makes him
not only know
that he exists but also feel
that his existence
is special, more special
than the tree or the woman, or the way Wordsworth
puts it, a poet
is A MAN PLEASED
WITH HIS OWN PASSIONS AND VOLITIONS, AND WHO
REJOICES MORE THAN OTHER MEN
IN THE SPIRIT OF LIFE
THAT IS IN HIM. Being a good Romantic poet
was a lot

like being a bad
boyfriend, and you could
get away with it
because the tree or the woman in the cottage
never turned to Wordsworth to say, William,
you are making this all about yourself, what about
my feelings? I don't know
what it means to be
a good poet today, but everyday
I try to know and fail. What's interesting
to me is that this way of perceiving
a tree or a woman in a cottage
is thought
to be modern, that it's
A modern problem. But I can't imagine
how we might think in a way that doesn't divide the world
into me and not me, even though
in books some philosophers
try to think a way out of
this problem, try to dissolve
the Cartesian subject. But did a medieval monk
not understand himself as a subject
in relationship to a world
of objects? The answer is beyond
my field of expertise. If this were

a game show, I would now ask to call a friend.
I would call my friend,
Jim Knowles, a medievalist. Hi, Jim, this
is Maggie. Does a medieval subject
divide the world into me and not me? Even if
he doesn't, Jim,
the language does, I would say,
maybe just proving
my own modernity. Grammar
divides us. When I was walking
to class the day we were
to discuss Stein, I was
a little nervous. POETRY & GRAMMAR
is maybe a difficult essay, I thought. Then I thought,
it's not that difficult. I still don't like
TENDER BUTTONS and I don't
really want to talk
about it, but it's really
famous and everybody thinks
it's important, I thought, so I need to talk
about it,
I thought. I do still like LIFTING BELLY,
because it says so many
dirty things
without ever saying

dirty things, I thought. Does this make me
a simple person, I wondered. I didn't
care and decided I would use
LIFTING BELLY instead of TENDER BUTTONS
to help explain Stein's essay. I had to be convinced
of what I was talking about
while trying to explain what Stein meant
in POETRY & GRAMMAR,
to explain what she meant
when she wrote,
I TOO FELT IN ME THE NEED
OF MAKING IT BE A THING
THAT COULD BE NAMED
WITHOUT USING ITS NAME. I had to use
a poem I liked. When I walked
into class
I was surprised that Collie said
she liked Stein and I think
Polina also said
she liked Stein, or
maybe it was Arielle. I thought
then that I worried too much about students
not liking Stein. I worried too much about students
being scared of things that I think
are maybe difficult, though neither

Collie nor Polina and/or Arielle said
if they had liked TENDER BUTTONS. Shelby said
she didn't get Stein, but Shelby always said
she didn't get things
when she did and
later when I read Shelby's paper
it was of course clear that Shelby got Stein,
really got Stein. I knew that
by the time we were through with Stein
we would have to understand
the difference between THINGS, THEIR NAMES, NOUNS, and NAMING
but first we had to understand
why Stein said
WHAT POETRY IS IT IS A STATE OF KNOWING AND FEELING A NAME
and how this connects to the idea
that a name is
A THING TO BE REMEMBERED. Or at least
I was interested in how names and memory
work together.
Of course
a name is a way to keep
a thing in the world
in yourself. We all know this
even if we haven't said this
to ourselves. We especially

know this
when we are college students
in love with someone eating a sandwich
on the other side of the cafeteria.
We say the person's name over and over and it makes us feel
a little bit like the person is with us
eating a sandwich but not enough
with us for us to get
bored and stop saying their
name. The ideas in Stein
aren't difficult. It's figuring out
why she says these things the way
she does that is maybe
difficult or maybe just
at first. But any college
student, even a student at
the business school, who
will never read
Stein, knows that this
is why people repeat
the name of someone
eating a sandwich
on the other
side of the cafeteria.
In class while teaching

Stein I kept repeating, MARIA,
I JUST MET A GIRL
NAMED MARIA, so that my students
would understand this idea, so that my students
would understand that
they already were
familiar with this
idea, though I'm not sure
if it was helpful. Do young
people still know WEST SIDE
STORY? I don't really
know WEST SIDE STORY, but
I know this line
from this song. At home Gina and
I sing this line
in the voices
of our dogs, in the voices
we have made up
for our dogs, but, as I often say
in class after I say
something irrelevant,
that's neither here
nor there. In any case,
I always want to simply explain
complex things without

simplifying the complexities
and that's why I
can't stop using the line
from WEST SIDE STORY
in class. But Stein's idea is maybe
more complex
than I make it. As a child,
Stein says, she found her much older
brother's love poems,
and that's how she learned about
poetry. In her description of
her brother's poem
the words Stein's brother wrote don't
make the girl present,
instead they make other things present.
In the poem Stein's brother
says his love has made him
see everything
in the world differently. He says he
HAD OFTEN SAT AND LOOKED AT ANY
LITTLE SQUARE OF GRASS
AND IT HAD BEEN
JUST A SQUARE OF
GRASS AS GRASS IS,
BUT NOW HE WAS IN LOVE AND SO

THE LITTLE SQUARE OF GRASS WAS ALL
FILLED WITH BIRDS AND BEES AND BUTTERFLIES,
THE DIFFERENCE WAS
WHAT WAS LOVE.
Stein says, BEING IN LOVE MADE
HIM MAKE POETRY, AND POETRY MADE HIM FEEL
THE THINGS AND THEIR NAMES, AND SO
I REPEAT NOUNS
ARE POETRY. Only now
in reading this again
and writing it with my own
hands here is it clear
to me that love
doesn't make him perceive things better, doesn't make
his sense perceptions sharper, but instead
love makes him write poetry and poetry makes
HIM FEEL THE THINGS AND
THEIR NAMES. If love makes him want
to write poetry, does that mean
love makes him want to feel
things but love
needs poetry
to make him feel those things
through nouns? I'm not
sure if Stein thinks

poetry makes us feel things
that are here in the world,
or things that are here in poetry.
What I mean is
that before love
IT HAD BEEN JUST A SQUARE OF GRASS AS GRASS IS
for Stein's brother
but when Stein says
GRASS AS GRASS IS
does she mean
the GRASS before love was grass perceived
'correctly,' GRASS AS GRASS IS
verifiable through our sense perceptions,
and that after love, once love makes us
write poetry, the grass full
of names and nouns is only the grass
in the poem, not the grass in
the world? I'm not exactly
sure because she says,
POETRY MADE HIM FEEL THE THINGS AND THEIR NAMES
which makes me think that Stein's
brother doesn't feel things
in the world but only words
in the poem, that he's feeling the things
through the words, but I'm not sure

because Stein puts THE THINGS first
in the sentence and then says THEIR NAMES. Is he really
feeling things in the world or
only things as nouns
in the poem? And if he is only feeling nouns
in a poem is it possible
that this also allows him to feel
things in the world, does poetry open him
to the world or only
to a world of words? It was a person
in the world, a person he loved
who excited him enough to want to feel things
and wanting to feel things
led to making
poetry, to making a poetry
that is a space in which to be
excited about things and their names. So is love
the link between the world and poetry?
Maybe the point is that
repeatedly reading Stein
creates more ways
to continue thinking
about how the world and poetry need
one another, might need one another, more ways
to try to understand

the link between
the world and poetry, more ways to understand
how the link between the world
and poetry explains what it means
to be alive, explains what
it feels like to be alive, which is just
another way of saying I'm
not exactly sure what Stein
means. Her syntax here
is ambiguous. What worries me most
about my love of poetry
is that I can't always understand
what it has to do
with being alive in the world, alive in a world
that seems more and more
about death, the death
of the world itself. I like Stein's definition
of poetry
because it's what poetry
sometimes feels like to me. It's why
I like poetry with
lots of concrete nouns,
especially if they are concrete nouns
that are surprising and
unexpected in poetry, the kind of nouns

that are the names of things
in the world
but not the names of things
that usually appear in poetry. It's a beautiful
thing I think when a poem
names something
that hasn't until then appeared in poetry
and in naming the thing
that isn't a thing
usually or ever to be named in poetry the poem
names the thing but also
still goes on being poetry. In those
moments it feels to me
as though poetry has just made itself
bigger to hold the world that always
is getting bigger and bigger. Maybe
it's wrong for me to think
this because Stein seems to be saying
that poetry makes the world bigger, but I can't
really control my thinking. I like
to think
all these things
about poetry.
It feels good, when most things
in the world

right now
feel bad. What is clear
in any case is that love doesn't
ever make Stein's brother sing,
I JUST MET A GIRL NAMED MARIA
like I said in class. Maybe
the most important thing in Stein and
something I think we did work
out in class, maybe the most important thing
Stein says is that names
can get old, can stop working,
that nouns meant
to make us feel
the things
stop working
as a way for us to feel
the things
because as Stein says
by the time
Whitman starts writing,
WE WHO HAD KNOWN THE NAMES SO LONG DID NOT GET A THRILL
FROM JUST KNOWING THEM.
By the mid-nineteenth century
nouns, Stein thinks, are worn out
and that's why Whitman thinks

to use nouns in a new way. Now notice Stein
uses the word THRILL,
a word that means
the vibrating or quivering of anything tangible
or visible; acute tremulousness, as of a sound;
a vibration, throbbing,
a tremor. In other words, she uses a word,
which is almost a dirty word. A word, which if we think
about it long enough, signifies anything
that works on us like
a personal massager. I have
on very rare occasions experienced
poetry this way,
very rarely, but the few times
that I have, it was
beautiful and it made me keep looking
for words for my poems and in other people's poems
to THRILL me and other
people. And maybe this is what reading
and writing poetry really is,
a search for words that thrill us, a search for the words
that will make us tremble
in the presence of all that is in the world,
even if all that is in the world is just
words in a poem. This can't

be true, though, because there are too many poems that mean
to be something other
than a thrill. I would like it
to be sometimes true. The poet's job for Stein is to make sure
that the thrill
is never gone and when the thrill starts to fade
the way we use language and the way
we make poetry
has to change. So, for example,
if we sing I JUST MET
A GIRL NAMED MARIA and it feels
instead like we are singing
MARIA, WHERE ARE MY KEYS? poets
need to do something. Stein says
she COMMENCED TRYING TO DO
SOMETHING IN TENDER BUTTONS
ABOUT THIS THING. And though I like
what Stein is saying here, TENDER BUTTONS
doesn't thrill me, but LIFTING BELLY
does. Like TENDER BUTTONS, LIFTING BELLY tries
to find A WAY OF NAMING THINGS
THAT WOULD NOT INVENT NAMES, BUT MEAN
NAMES WITHOUT NAMING THEM, but LIFTING BELLY
is about Gertrude
trying to tell us

what it's like to have sex
with Alice while
never saying THIS IS WHAT IT'S
LIKE TO HAVE SEX WITH ALICE,
but making us all know
that she is telling
us what it's
like to have sex
with Alice. TENDER BUTTONS, on the other hand,
is about mutton.
Sex, I assume, is, for most
people, more thrilling than
mutton, especially for vegetarians.
Stein, I also assume, knows that THRILL
as a word, has something
to do with sex. It's a word
that has to do with trembling,
with piercing, with penetrating, so I'm not sure
why she thinks TENDER BUTTONS,
which is a book
of poetry about mutton
would be THRILLING
but of course who wouldn't say
that LIFTING BELLY
isn't THRILLING? And LIFTING

BELLY as a name falls into a long
tradition of NAMES WITHOUT
NAMING THEM because that's how people
seem to have always talked
about sex because sex
is like love and it makes
you want to make poems,
to name things
without naming them.
Like for instance, on the internet I found
all these names that weren't
in poems and weren't made by poets, but sound
like they want to be
in a poem like LIFTING BELLY,
names like, CURTAIN TWITCHING, ENTANGLING
THE LOWER BEARDS, FIDGETING THE MIDGET IN BRIDGET,
FIXING THE CLAP FLAP, GOING HEELS-TO-JESUS,
and so on. To be fair,
there also were names
that seemed to belong
in TENDER BUTTONS. Names
that made
LIFTING BELLY sound
like mutton. For example, MASHING THE FAT,
HAVING HOT PUDDING FOR SUPPER,

LOCKING LEGS AND SWAPPING GRAVY,
RUMMAGING IN THE ROOT CELLAR,
AND PUDDLE-SNUGGLING. When LIFTING BELLY
sounds like lifting mutton,
I have to say, I don't feel like
lifting anything. In class I didn't say
any of these things
because I was
trying to be appropriate, though sometimes
it's difficult to teach poetry as it actually is
and not say things
that some people
would think weren't appropriate
to say in a college classroom, but I didn't
invent the history of poetry, I'm just
the messenger. I can't avoid
these things and still show my students
what really is
in the world and in poetry. When we talked
about the phrase LIFTING BELLY
as a way of naming something without using its name
I for a second
worried that the students wouldn't
understand what LIFTING BELLY meant and for a second
I was tempted

to do an Elvis pelvis
which maybe would not have been appropriate for me
to do as a professor and
luckily I stopped myself. I reminded myself
that these were college students
and they were thinking mostly about
LIFTING BELLY all the time
because that's a lot of what it means
to be a college
student and I don't need to spell
anything out. These things can exist
as a wink wink and everyone
understands. We looked at a poem in TENDER BUTTONS and
I was honest
and told my students
that I didn't
GET Tender Buttons and I said that
when I use the word GET
I mean I didn't FEEL TENDER BUTTONS and Stein
herself said that the poem
was supposed to make me FEEL the things and
their names. I asked my students
if anyone GOT TENDER BUTTONS and Ruth Anne who
was always generous to poems
and to words was able to show us how

she thought A LITTLE MONKEY GOES
LIKE A DONKEY was for Stein a new way
of saying DOG. And I was grateful for Ruth Anne
because she showed us
very quickly how TENDER BUTTONS worked. And to be honest
I liked that passage because I have
a little dog and I often call him MONKEY.
What's clear here is that there's
a difference between understanding and
feeling. I understand
TENDER BUTTONS, but I don't
feel it. It doesn't THRILL me. The difference
between TENDER BUTTONS and LIFTING BELLY
illustrates the Cartesian
mind/body split, or the problem
for me is that TENDER BUTTONS asks
readers to think instead of feel
how Stein names things
in new ways. She wants to renew
perception, but perception in TENDER BUTTONS
is defined as seeing. Our eyes
often don't let us
feel things but instead help us
know things. That's why apprehend is
a word sometimes used

in philosophy to describe
how a person sees
an object. So a writer might say,
THE FACULTY OF VISION APPREHENDS OBJECTS
IN THE WORLD. It's also the word
we use to describe
something the police do.
So the woman on the news might say, POLICE OFFICERS
APPREHENDED THREE TEENAGE
SUSPECTS TODAY. In our world then
we risk thinking that to know something is
also to capture something, to control it. For this reason
it seems to me
that perceiving something
only through sight might
not be the same
as the THRILL of names and naming
Stein describes
in POETRY & GRAMMAR. To be thrilled by something
is to lose control
in some small way. I've been careful
most of my life
not to say
any of this
in public because

everyone it seems
loves TENDER BUTTONS and
up until now
I have been worried that
if people knew
I didn't like TENDER BUTTONS
they would think
I was stupid
but recently I've started
to care less
about whether or not
people think I am stupid. I think
this means I am finally
no longer a girl, but a woman. This only took
forty-five years. I don't like TENDER BUTTONS.
I don't like TENDER BUTTONS because
I don't feel TENDER BUTTONS. It doesn't
thrill me. There, I said it.
In high school I had an English teacher, Mr. Bob Wicke,
who would do things
a teacher wasn't supposed to do,
especially in Catholic high school. And that's why
we liked him, that's why some
of us liked him, why I liked
him. For instance, one day just as

we were settling into
our seats, Bob closed
the classroom door and
with a grand gesture turned off the intercom,
so that we all knew
Sr. Donna couldn't listen into the room. He then
turned to us and said,
CLASS, THERE IS NO GOD,
and laughed and then he asked us
to open our books,
as if nothing had happened, as if
he had said
nothing at all. At the time
we were all
also in a religion class
called CHRISTIAN MARRIAGE HONORS because
we were HONORS students
so we were always separated
from the regular students
except for gym. In CHRISTIAN MARRIAGE HONORS
Joe Parks was my husband.
He and I had to plan our wedding and
create a budget to furnish our future house
using catalogs we brought
from home. We also had to take

a written test
on all available birth control methods,
a requirement imposed on the school
by the state of New Jersey.
Even though we had to show
that we knew everything about each birth control method,
we had also to show that
as Catholics we knew we were not to use
any birth control methods
except for abstinence, but as Catholics
we also knew what had happened
to the Virgin Mary
when she, like all of us
in CHRISTIAN MARRIAGE HONORS, wasn't having sex.
In CHRISTIAN MARRIAGE HONORS we also
had to take a written test
on HOMOSEXUALITY,
on the OFFICIAL ROMAN CATHOLIC position
on HOMOSEXUALITY. For some reason
we all failed the HOMOSEXUALITY
test. Mrs. Larkin, who had a theology degree
from Princeton, was very angry
that we had all failed. Of course we were
all confused as to why someone with a degree
from Princeton was stuck teaching us

about HOMOSEXUALITY but we were also very
confused about why we had failed.
As Mrs. Larkin reiterated to us what
she believed to be a subtly nuanced
theological position I remember
all of us looking at each other in confusion
and shouting, BUT THAT'S WHAT I WROTE!
I imagine it didn't look
good, if the entire CHRISTIAN MARRIAGE
HONORS class failed the HOMOSEXUALITY
test, so she made us
retake it. Of course, we all passed.
A year earlier, Joe and I
had been in Rich Wicke's, Bob Wicke's
younger brother's, English class. I had a crush
on Rich Wicke because
he was a poet and because he said things like
ALL WOMEN SHOULD BECOME LESBIANS
and because
he and his wife
had named their daughter Adrienne
after a very famous lesbian poet,
who I had never heard of before. Rich Wicke,
when he should have been teaching us John Donne or
Andrew Marvell poems, instead

often spent the fifty minute
class period explaining
the world to us. For instance, he explained to us
how a traditional wedding ceremony
symbo ized the transference of property, i.e. the woman,
from one man to another and
that by taking her husband's name
a woman was showing
the world that she was
her husband's property. Knowing these things
complicated CHRISTIAN MARRIAGE HONORS
for Joe and me. He and I wanted
to have the kind of marriage that abolished
all signs of the wife
as property of the husband.
We had the idea that instead of me
taking Joe's last name,
we would both
change our last name
to a new name, a combination of both our last names,
Zurparkski, but when
we told Mrs. Larkin
that we wanted to be the Zurparkski family
instead of Mr. and Mrs. Joe Parks,
she said it would be fine, but only if we wrote

an essay about our reasons
for going against tradition. Of course we immediately
agreed to be Mr. and Mrs. Joe Parks.
No one really
likes writing
essays. We all
thought Rich Wicke had more integrity than
his brother, Bob, because although
both men espoused feminist
ideas in class, Rich Wicke didn't
dye his hair blonde, or wear
tight pants, or go
to a tanning salon, or have
a live-in girlfriend, who was much
younger than he was. Bob's pants were so tight
that we had to make jokes
in the hallway
behind his back
about the state
of his testicles. These things made us think
that when Bob
was telling us
men are awful, when he was telling us
that we should all
become lesbians, he was also

maybe warning us
about himself. A pair of pants
made us consider all of this. In other words,
we already knew
that FORM IS ONLY
AN EXTENSION OF CONTENT, though
we didn't know
we knew it. One day in Bob's class
we read Sartre's
NO EXIT aloud. Bob picked Kathryn,
one of the only cheerleaders
in the Honors program, to read the part
of Estelle, the straight woman. He chose me
to play Inez, the lesbian, and
he himself read
the part of Garcin, the straight man. Or maybe
Kathryn and I volunteered to play
the parts. I don't
remember. But for fifty minutes
I got to make passes
at Kathryn, Kathryn got
to make passes at Bob, and Bob got
to make passes at me. Years later
I learned that the play
was about how the self struggles

when it sees
itself as an object
from the point of view of
another self. Back then, though,
in Bob Wicke's class
the play for me was about the thrill
of being seen by other people
in the same way
I saw and felt myself. NO EXIT
created a feeling of freedom
in my world, a freedom hidden behind
the closed doors
of Bob's classroom. Ten years ago
I learned from a friend, who had also been in
Bob's class, that Bob
had lost his job, that he had been put
on trial. The local paper
reported that Bob had received
sexual favors from a female
student in exchange for
a good grade. When I told my father,
who was always the one to go
to parent/teacher conferences, he said
he wasn't surprised. He, too, had seen
Bob's pants. On Facebook

another friend said she didn't care
about the news. Bob's class
had saved her life. I understood what she meant.
He and Rich had saved my life.
When I think about Bob, I still
get mad at him
for not realizing it was a problem
that though he told us
there were many
good books written
by women, he never taught
a single one of them. When I get mad
at Bob for this, I wonder
if there's something
wrong with me
that this is the thing
I feel mad at him for. I get that he did
many other things wrong, but I feel
this one. It's hard not to think
my feeling, then, is self-interested,
especially as I type.

AFTER-WORDS

A LINE OF FLIGHT
A CONVERSATION WITH
MAGDALENA ZURAWSKI

Greetings! Thank you for talking to us about your process today! Can you introduce yourself, in a way that you would choose?

I'm a poet and teacher, living in Athens, GA.

Why are you a poet/writer/artist?

Because it allows conversations to happen. Conversations that need to happen. Conversations that otherwise wouldn't happen.

When did you decide you were a poet/writer/artist (and/or: do you feel comfortable calling yourself a poet/writer/artist, what other titles or affiliations do you prefer/feel are more accurate)?

I woke up one morning at the age of 13 and went to my desk and wrote a poem after having a strange dream. From then on I felt dedicated to poetry.

What's a "poet" (or "writer" or "artist") anyway?

A poet is someone who constructs forms out of words.

What do you see as your cultural and social role (in the literary / artistic / creative community and beyond)?

I take teaching seriously. The classroom for me was a problematic but life-changing space, a line of flight. I feel obligated to make it that kind of space for my students. Sometimes I fall short, but I try. I take local and state politics seriously after the GA legislature made guns legal in my classroom. I work on campaigns etc. My motivation there is making sure there's some sort of viable reality for my students to inherit. It seems like we're losing on that front at the moment, but I'll be working on campaigns here in GA over the coming year.

Talk about the process or instinct to move these poems (or your work in general) as independent entities into a body of work. How and why did this happen?

This piece is what I've been calling an essay with line breaks. Given that my classroom has been under attack in several ways, it felt important to take the experience of teaching and my relationship with my students seriously, to externalize everything that is taking place for me when I enter the classroom. It seemed important, too, that my students might be able to read it.

Speaking of monikers, what does your title represent? How was it generated?

When I was a grad student at Duke I got to study and to know Fred Moten. One day, I think in seminar, he mentioned that he wanted to teach a course called "Don't Be Scared." The reading list would be all those huge works of literature people often are too scared to read. I remember The Making of Americans being on the list and Pamela. The discussion of this fantasy course was an aside, if I remember correctly, but something that I think about often because "Don't Be Scared" is in many ways the perfect classroom philosophy.

Students are scared of not understanding things, of appearing to not understand something, etc. My job is to let them know they don't have to be scared. They can think out loud, be wrong, confused, etc. and it's all important and helpful for the work we're doing together. When I started to write this piece about teaching, I was fixated on a memory of having to get students past the word Cartesian on the first day of a poetics class. That word felt like an opportunity because it turns what is essentially at this point a cliché ("I think therefore I am") into a capitalized adjective, an intimidating academic term that seems to stand for a whole world beyond what a student who is first encountering philosophy, theory, or poetics thinks she knows. But of course people who have never even set foot on a college campus have likely heard the phrase "I think therefore I am" as a punchline on a 70s sitcom or something. I bet there are even some business majors who have heard the phrase. Anyhow, it's a good first lesson in showing students that they don't need to be scared of not knowing something. Cartesian is just a name you don't know for an idea you do know. Don't be scared.

What does this book DO (as much as what it says or contains)? What would be the best possible outcome for this book? What might it do in the world, and how will its presence as an object facilitate your creative role in your community and beyond? What are your hopes for this book, and for your practice?

This book is an acknowledgement that my students are the people with whom I think and talk about art most intensely. The economic situation of poets in America has created a kind of diasporic poetry community. Many of us are bound to some campus. And even if we're in major cities, we can't really afford to live in neighborhoods alongside each other. Even in NY it seems no one can afford to live around The Poetry Project anymore. NY poets have a long commute to reach what used to be a neighborhood's poetry space. So this piece is an effort to take seriously the community I create with my students, to take seriously the thinking about poetry that happens with and through them. They are on a daily basis my poetry friends. My other poetry family is less integrated into my daily life.

ABOUT THE AUTHOR

MAGDALENA ZURAWSKI is the author of **The Tiniest Muzzle Sings Songs of Freedom** (Wave Books 2019), the novel **The Bruise**, which won the Ronald Sukenick Award from FC2 in 2008 and a LAMBDA literary award in 2009, and the collection of poems ***Companion Animal,*** which was published by Litmus Press in 2015 and won a Norma Faber First Book Award from the Poetry Society of America. She attended Brown University where she studied with poets Rosmarie and Keith Waldrop, C.D. Wright, and Peter Gizzi. She has lived in Berlin, New York, Philadelphia, San Francisco, and Durham, NC where she ran the Minor American Reading Series. She is currently Assistant Professor of English and Creative Writing at the University of Georgia.

ABOUT THE COVER ART:

The Operating System 2019 chapbooks, in both digital and print, feature art from Heidi Reszies. The work is from a series entitled "Collected Objects & the Dead Birds I Did Not Carry Home," which are mixed media collages with encaustic on 8 x 8 wood panel, made in 2018.

Heidi writes: "This series explores objects/fragments of material culture—how objects occupy space, and my relationship to them or to their absence."

ABOUT THE ARTIST:

Heidi Reszies is a poet/transdisciplinary artist living in Richmond, Virginia. Her visual art is included in the National Museum of Women in the Arts CLARA Database of Women Artists. She teaches letterpress printing at the Virginia Commonwealth University School of the Arts, and is the creator/curator of Artifact Press. Her poetry collection titled *Illusory Borders* is forthcoming from The Operating System in 2019, and now available for pre-order. Her collection titled *Of Water & Other Soft Constructions* was selected by Samiya Bashir as the winner of the Anhinga Press 2018 Robert Dana Prize for Poetry (forthcoming in 2019).

Find her at heidireszies.com

WHY PRINT DOCUMENT?

The Operating System uses the language "print document" to differentiate from the book-object as part of our mission to distinguish the act of documentation-in-book-FORM from the act of publishing as a backwards-facing replication of the book's agentive *role* as it may have appeared the last several centuries of its history. Ultimately, I approach the book as TECHNOLOGY: one of a variety of printed documents (in this case, bound) that humans have invented and in turn used to archive and disseminate ideas, beliefs, stories, and other evidence of production.

Ownership and use of printing presses and access to (or restriction of printed materials) has long been a site of struggle, related in many ways to revolutionary activity and the fight for civil rights and free speech all over the world. While (in many countries) the contemporary quotidian landscape has indeed drastically shifted in its access to platforms for sharing information and in the widespread ability to "publish" digitally, even with extremely limited resources, the importance of publication on physical media has not diminished. In fact, this may be the most critical time in recent history for activist groups, artists, and others to insist upon learning, establishing, and encouraging personal and community documentation practices. Hear me out.

With The OS's print endeavors I wanted to open up a conversation about this: the ultimately radical, transgressive act of creating PRINT /DOCUMENTATION in the digital age. It's a question of the archive, and of history: who gets to tell the story, and what evidence of our life, our behaviors, our experiences are we leaving behind? We can know little to nothing about the future into which we're leaving an unprecedentedly digital document trail — but we can be assured that publications, government agencies, museums, schools, and other institutional powers that be will continue to leave BOTH a digital and print version of their production for the official record. Will we?

As a (rogue) anthropologist and long time academic, I can easily pull up many accounts about how lives, behaviors, experiences — how THE STORY of a time or place — was pieced together using the deep study of correspondence, notebooks, and other physical documents which are no longer the norm in many lives and practices. As we move our creative behaviors towards digital note taking, and even audio and video, what can we predict about future technology that is in any way assuring that our stories will be accurately told – or told at all? How will we leave these things for the record?

In these documents we say: WE WERE HERE, WE EXISTED, WE HAVE A DIFFERENT STORY

- Lynne DeSilva-Johnson [ELÆ], Founder/Managing Editor,
THE OPERATING SYSTEM, Brooklyn NY 2019

SELECTED RECENT AND FORTHCOMING OS PRINT/DOCUMENTS

ARK HIVE-Marthe Reed [2019]
A Bony Framework for the Tangible Universe-D. Allen [kin(d)*, 2019]
Y - Lori Anderson Moseman
Śnienie / Dreaming - Marta Zelwan/Krystyna Sakowicz,
(Polish-English/dual-language) trans. Victoria Miluch [glossarium, 2019]
Opera on TV-James Brunton [kin(d)*, 2019]
Alparegho: Pareil-À-Rien / Alparegho, Like Nothing Else - Hélène Sanguinetti
(French-English/dual-language), trans. Ann Cefola [glossarium, 2019]
Hall of Waters-Berry Grass [kin(d)*, 2019]
High Tide Of The Eyes - Bijan Elahi (Farsi-English/dual-language)
trans. Rebecca Ruth Gould and Kayvan Tahmasebian [glossarium, 2019]
I Made for You a New Machine and All it Does is Hope - Richard Lucyshyn [2019]
Illusory Borders-Heidi Reszies [2019]
Transitional Object-Adrian Silbernagel [kin(d)*, 2019]
A Year of Misreading the Wildcats [2019]
An Absence So Great and Spontaneous It Is Evidence of Light - Anne Gorrick [2018]
The Book of Everyday Instruction - Chloe Bass [2018]
Executive Orders Vol. II - a collaboration with the Organism for Poetic Research [2018]
One More Revolution - Andrea Mazzariello [2018]
The Suitcase Tree - Filip Marinovich [2018]
Chlorosis - Michael Flatt and Derrick Mund [2018]
Sussuros a Mi Padre - Erick Sáenz [2018]
Sharing Plastic - Blake Nemec [2018]
The Book of Sounds - Mehdi Navid (Farsi dual language, trans. Tina Rahimi) [2018]
In Corpore Sano : Creative Practice and the Challenged Body [Anthology, 2018];
Lynne DeSilva-Johnson and Jay Besemer, co-editors
Abandoners - Lesley Ann Wheeler [2018]
Jazzercise is a Language - Gabriel Ojeda-Sague [2018]
Return Trip / Viaje Al Regreso - Israel Dominguez;
(Spanish-English dual language) trans. Margaret Randall [2018]
Born Again - Ivy Johnson [2018]
Attendance - Rocío Carlos and Rachel McLeod Kaminer [2018]
Singing for Nothing - Wally Swist [2018]
The Ways of the Monster - Jay Besemer [2018]

THE 2019 OS CHAPBOOK SERIES

PRINT TITLES:

Vela. - Knar Gavin
[零] A Phantom Zero - Ryu Ando
Don't Be Scared - Magdalena Zurawski
Re:Verses - Kristina Darling & Chris Campanioni

***

DIGITAL TITLES:

American Policy Player's Guide and Dream Book - Rachel Zolf
The George Oppen Memorial BBQ - Eric Benick
Flight Of The Mothman - Gyasi Hall
Mass Transitions - Sue Landers
The Grass Is Greener When The Sun Is Yellow - Sarah Rosenthal & Valerie Witte
From Being Things, To Equalities In All - Joe Milazzo
These Deals Won't Last Forever - Sasha Amari Hawkins
Ventriloquy - Bonnie Emerick
A Period Of Non-Enforcement - Lindsay Miles
Quantum Mechanics : Memoirs Of A Quark - Brad Baumgartner
Hara-Kiri On Monkey Bars - Anna Hoff

***

PLEASE SEE OUR FULL CATALOG
FOR FULL LENGTH VOLUMES AND PREVIOUS CHAPBOOK SERIES:
HTTPS://SQUAREUP.COM/STORE/THE-OPERATING-SYSTEM/

THE 2019 SERIES MARKS OUR 7TH AND FINAL SPRING 4-BOOK SERIES
THANK YOU TO ALL THE WONDERFUL CREATORS BEHIND THESE TITLES

CHAPBOOK SERIES 2018 : TALES
Greater Grave - Jacq Greyja; Needles of Itching Feathers - Jared Schlickling;
Want-Catcher - Adra Raine; We, The Monstrous - Mark DuCharme

CHAPBOOK SERIES 2017 : INCANTATIONS
featuring original cover art by Barbara Byers
sp. - Susan Charkes; Radio Poems - Jeffrey Cyphers Wright;
Fixing a Witch/Hexing the Stitch - Jacklyn Janeksela;
cosmos a personal voyage by carl sagan ann druyan steven sotor and me - Connie Mae Oliver

CHAPBOOK SERIES 2016: OF SOUND MIND
*featuring the quilt drawings of Daphne Taylor
Improper Maps - Alex Crowley; While Listening - Alaina Ferris;
Chords - Peter Longofono; Any Seam or Needlework - Stanford Cheung

CHAPBOOK SERIES 2015: OF SYSTEMS OF
*featuring original cover art by Emma Steinkraus
Cyclorama - Davy Knittle; The Sensitive Boy Slumber Party Manifesto - Joseph
Cuillier; Neptune Court - Anton Yakovlev; Schema - Anurak Saelow

CHAPBOOK SERIES 2014: BY HAND
Pull, A Ballad - Maryam Parhizkar;
Can You See that Sound - Jeff Musillo
Executive Producer Chris Carter - Peter Milne Greiner;
Spooky Action at a Distance - Gregory Crosby;

CHAPBOOK SERIES 2013: WOODBLOCK
*featuring original prints from Kevin William Reed
Strange Coherence - Bill Considine; The Sword of Things - Tony Hoffman;
Talk About Man Proof - Lancelot Runge / John Kropa;
An Admission as a Warning Against the Value of Our Conclusions - Alexis Quinlan

DOC U MENT
/däkyəmənt/

First meant "instruction" or "evidence," whether written or not.

noun - a piece of written, printed, or electronic matter that provides information or evidence or that serves as an official record
verb - record (something) in written, photographic, or other form
synonyms - paper - deed - record - writing - act - instrument

[*Middle English, precept, from Old French, from Latin documentum, example, proof, from docre, to teach; see dek- in Indo-European roots.*]

Who is responsible for the manufacture of value?

Based on what supercilious ontology have we landed in a space where we vie against other creative people in vain pursuit of the fleeting credibilities of the scarcity economy, rather than freely collaborating and sharing openly with each other in ecstatic celebration of MAKING?

While we understand and acknowledge the economic pressures and fear-mongering that threatens to dominate and crush the creative impulse, we also believe that *now more than ever we have the tools to relinquish agency via cooperative means,* fueled by the fires of the Open Source Movement.

Looking out across the invisible vistas of that rhizomatic parallel country we can begin to see our community beyond constraints, in the place where intention meets resilient, proactive, collaborative organization.

Here is a document born of that belief, sown purely of imagination and will.
When we document we assert. We print to make real, to reify our being there.
When we do so with mindful intention to address our process, to open our work to others,
to create beauty in words in space, to respect and acknowledge the strength of the page we now hold
physical, a thing in our hand... we remind ourselves that, like Dorothy: *we had the power all along, my dears.*

THE PRINT! DOCUMENT SERIES

is a project of
the trouble with bartleby
in collaboration with
the operating system

www.ingramcontent.com/pod-product-compliance
Lightning Source LLC
Chambersburg PA
CBHW080028130526
44591CB00037B/2708